LOVE'S BEYOND

LOVE'S BEYOND

Akanksha Chaudhary

Ocean Paperbacks
A Division of Ocean Books Pvt. Ltd.
ISO 9001:2008 Publishers

Published by
Ocean Paperbacks
A Division of Ocean Books Pvt. Ltd.
4/19 Asaf Ali Road,
New Delhi-110 002 (INDIA)
e-mail: info@oceanbooks.in

ISBN 978-81-8430-183-0
Love's Beyond
by Akanksha Chaudhary

Edition
First, 2013

Price
Rs. 150.00 (Rs. One Hundred Fifty only)

Printed at
Bhanu Printers, Delhi

Contents

There comes a point of time in life where you are automatically, symphony-lead by a passion so strong that the world around you ceases to breathe. Such is the organism, soul creates when breath is withdrawn from societal obligations and a peaceful seclusion is curtained for the unknown.

The First Memory of Love

Nothing ever gets completed without the blessings of our loved ones. And my family's forever present love and care has always allowed me to heartily lead my words to the world at large.

The first memory of love in my life was when, while walking in a park with my dad one day, he told me with greatest delight, "When you really want someone in your life from the deepest core of yearning in your heart, then ultimately you unite with that person one day".

My dad had met my mom in a library as she was taking classes as a lecturer in one of the Delhi University colleges. It was their first meeting through arranged marriage procedure. He said, "When I looked at her, she looked up at me and passed a gentle smile. And I knew she was the one."

Now 31 years later, I see them and they are still the same kids in love. They still have differences in opinions, but does that lessen the love? Never!

Nobody grows up in love too, I learnt, instead you grow yourself again. The others accept you the way you are and love you for that. Though for your improvements, they would themselves face any amount of difficulties.

Then my brother was more than a brother to me. His place in my life was like that lamp that never takes its light off even when the wind blows it off. He grew up as a guy who would do anything for his lady love, just like he did for his family. So when love came to him, I was more than sure about what true love really is. It's about being different yet similar in so many ways and means that your hearts never can stay apart despite the busyness in the work web.

Arman and G, the coolest love couple as I call them, made intense the idea of soul-mates in my soul.

From that day onwards, I knew all the thoughts I had about love would come true one day. Though the path may be shaky or lead to weaker grounds, but the one way, that is your own salvation path, truly shows up one day. I grew up believing that love happens and when it does, it stays – Always!

Such was the day of my love in the month of December 2010 when I met my love. It was love at first sight. And again, it was the laughter followed by endless smiles. I knew I wanted to see that smile at the end of every day to come.

Love is never a change you simply want to seek, but it's the change without which you can't live.

Let love fill in your days like the energies from the universe.

❑

Love's Beyond

The beauty of words has been dispersed throughout the universe and picked up from the multiplicities of emotions experienced, seen, known, developed and created by men. The day by day growing of a person when in love is a special phase not only because it makes any person feel elated and carefree or simply because it's the most beautiful feeling in the world but because as we involve ourselves into the feelings of being able to love somebody, we either grow or deteriorate ourselves completely. If we try to strike a balance, then we develop our emotions from the external sources that in true love might create obstacles of nature much known to men and women alike.

'Beyond' element in love represents the philosophy of a free spirit with which it lives its days, night and morn, celebrating phases of love.

People can truly live through and be in love only when they are clear from their souls that they are with the person they always truly wanted to be with. Any little doubt can spark off negativities so subtle that they might not ever get to know about it. It would untimely lead to feeling though in love and yet little disconnected with your lover.

At these times too, not everybody, that you may come across, seeks just love. There are reasons attached to each love story. Reasons, when sought through love that you truly care about, are much more substantial than just being parameters of desire that people talk about getting rid of.

So, in the journey of love while some of us become better persons, some enjoy being dependant. We keep travelling in our love circle back and forth. There is never one place. Even if you are disconnected with the world, you still grow in your love circle as a human being should. Some pursue love to fulfill the idea of soul mates, which is ever so appealing to those blessed to be with exactly the ones they always wanted, while some have to seek marriage for love. Marriage is great but, in the Indian context, it's not always the 'choice' of the girl or the boy. The trend is still changing, yet far from being inspirational.

This book discusses through soulful poetry, a deep observation of human emotions and their development; hence, representative of three phases of the concept called Love, i.e., Love Ideals, Love Memoirs and Love's Beyond.

❑

Foreword I

If love is all we needed, then all that Heaven knows would be redundant. Ultimately, love perseveres throughout on a trajectory we have no grasp or real concept of. Just a relative faith that it will prevail! It's a nourishment we all yearn for in some capacity. The freedom to choose whom we love and to what extent we choose to love them is boundless. Loving and wanting to be loved is a curious sort of freedom expressed elegantly and emphatically in Akanksha Chaudhary's 'Love's Beyond'. Tenderness was not in abundance in my early life up until the birth of my son, whereupon it flourished as though I was bathed in it everyday. It became familiar to me and I became comfortable with it, as my little boy's willingness to comply with the affection and attention I shared with him. Replacing what little I thought was left in me and finally accepting something missing had been found.

Insufferable as love at times may be, impatient and overwhelming, even pitiful. Akanksha seems to effortlessly convey an empathy and compassion in her poetry and word selection which, in my opinion, is truly extraordinarily rare. By 'rare' I mean a rawness close to the bone and marrow of a subject we are all familiar with, yet it piles softly in a wondrous aesthetic of combining words with what one feels to divulge what some of us find so desperately difficult to actualise. Heaven knows what love is. However, what follows in these next pages is what separates us from a bathing Ape or a wilderness of nothingness! We live to love, nothing else really matters at all.

All Bless.

—PJ. Tobin

Author of *'The Moon's Last Gasp'*

Foreword II

Oscar Wilde once famously said, "The mystery of love is greater than the mystery of death." Truly, no other human emotion or endeavour has generated as much thought, contemplation, despair, or art, as the feeling of love. Nonetheless, love remains an elusive entity, its ambiguity being particularly apparent in the context of volatile human relationships and emotions.

'Love's Beyond' by Akanksha Chaudhary is an exercise in understanding the multifarious shades and nuances of love. Divided into three parts, representing the three phases of love – Love Ideals, Love Memoirs and Love's Beyond, the book explores a poet's understanding of the concept of love in its often perplexing and interesting shades. The emotion of love has never been an easy one to traverse through, not just practically but figuratively too, especially in the realm of art, given its complex nature. But Chaudhary's endeavour is to shed some light on a fact of human life, which is as difficult to live without as it is to live with sometimes.

The re-discovery and re-understanding of love through the poetry in this book are meant for all those who seek to gain a certain grasp over the power of love and the hold it has on human life. Love has always been slightly nebulous, rare and precious in existence, and more so in this day and age, whence the fortitude and patience of human beings to bear adversities in life has worn thin. In such a scenario, many often give up hope on finding love for themselves, and forego even their belief in its existence. It is hoped that the book, through its poet's verses, re-affirms faith in that most delightful of human emotion called 'love'.

—**Dr. Bina Biswas**

Dr. Bina Biswas is a Professor of English Language and Communications at TRR Engineering College for Women, Jawaharlal Nehru Technological University, Hyderabad. She is an alumnus of the University of Delhi and has a Doctorate from Andhra University. She has carried out extensive research on Tagore's short stories and poems for over eight years. She writes short stories and poems and translates Tagore's poems and stories into English. Her stories have been published in different Indian and International journals. Her story 'Case of a Missing Shoe' has been selected for publication in The Indian Literature, Sahitya Akademi. Her research topics were Tagore's female protagonists in his short stories and his prose poems....respectively for M. Phil. and Ph.D. Presently, she is working on a biography on Rabindranath Tagore. She currently lives in Hyderabad with her husband and two children.

Love Ideals

The idea of love has always been nourishing somewhere deep inside our souls as we first came to this life and were received with joyful love by our family. Love is the highest ideal of our existence till date. No emotion more strong lies there in the empty lands or broken hearts that can take our breath away literally. With it or without it, we always unconsciously do things that ultimately represent love or cultivate love. The process you might stay unaware of and yet in your buried down closest of memories and thoughts, you always had dreams of how love should be, how it is and how you want it to be.

Love Ideals are innocent manifestations of a young soul trying to open its heart to the person they think could be the 'one love' for them. Ideas of love, dreams about love, and those lonely nights spent contemplating behaviour of the one you had a strong liking for and your hopes of finding somebody that would be a part of your own soul represents Love Ideals. These love ideals are deeply inculcated in our psychology as we grow up and we form an opinion of persons, things and emotions. It's your first take at the world other than your family.

Thus, one goes right from liking a person for something they do or something they reflect in their personality which we begin to idolize and then gradually love. This somebody is the one who matches the ideas of love you always had deep in your own soul.

As it is, love is the sweetest journey that one embarks upon

It's boulevards and turns barely the ending points

It's faults hardly visible enough through the light and it's charms, it's possibilities, it's never ending love ideals...

❑

To welcome change, one seeking love needs to be a 'careful chooser' than a mere 'chooser'.

Caught

Past ran away inhibitions
New came along all revelations
Tip-toed that chasing silence came to an end
Zigzag we ran, our traces we left a trail of...

Follow me, follow me not
For, past ran away my inhibitions
Speak to me, speak to me not
New I am, here for what you are...

Criss-cross, you kept your stare on the bed
Zip-zap and high flew away
Days never to end...

Be with me, be with me not
Have named you for divinity...

Hold me, hold me not
Life ties strong, to behold and belong

Ages, years and all crazy distances
What was never a possibility

Appeared what a mere dream
Created that in me a dream
Which has now come alive
With the beat of the heart
Where one cannot wait for the days to start...

❑

Choice or Two

If you ever have to get stuck by choice
Do that with the idea of celebrating life
Damn you forlorn flunks
Yes, that's what we were born to do

Failures are nothing but short of sights
You look at them and can see
What is needed

What you can't look at
Is beneath the puddle
Because you dig out what you want to hide

So fetch some hike and ride
Set on your plunging heights

Launch your pride weapons
Sousing them with your humour and wit
For nothing appeals mankind more than
A shared soak-able dip...

❑

Fay that brought Rain

Shower in the sky
And a beautiful pattern made

Shattered stays the lies
And our time just won't come

Mark a new beginning would this new sky route
Or trail down the inception to our last meeting?

Moments pass not so soon, longer seems the life
Made shorter it was once by our running steps..

When will you come, the wait is becoming dry
Tear down the sorrows, let my sun survive

Longer is the road much travelled already
Sits down on the edges the tired heart

Push it in what life needs to grow
Pull all that which is keeping it low

My heart is linked to yours
That is no one's business
Only for me to know

And for God to grow!
I believe,

Sky would be there one day
And a home shall be touched
When you and I will recognise our signs before our
life is plucked...

❑

Granted!

Thousand travelled distances
and several milestones sought after
Was going on with my life,
dealing it with a surface shine which added to the strife
Unknowingly came across to the purpose
I was born to behold, and embrace in life
Was shown the night light which shone
through your eyes and touched me through
Your smile...

Figure I couldn't how I fell in love
For you came along swiftly, re-assuring my beliefs
In what people call true love

Knew that you were there somewhere
The way I couldn't find on my own
But destiny charted circles and took me to where I
belong..

The more we chase, the more we compromise
The more we drift away from what was meant for us
The more we are pulled closer to that person

Carries us through the sky spreading
Thus the invisible hand of destiny
And brings us to the person
Who was meant to be loved
Not just for a lifetime but for many lives decided to be lived...

From the slumber I woke up for you hon
From the lost self I burgeoned to live out with you again...

Charm got over me and the love blind-folded
Madness drew far depth becoming brightened
Dreams for real were calling each second
And steps took me to you...

Such was the moment and such was the karma
That I was blessed to have you...
And there's only one thing I got to say to you
And that is that I will always love you...

❑

Hues of the Past

You and I, like the stars in the sky
far away from reality,
but giving some light...

You and I, like the wind in the rain
moving on ahead,
but caught up in the invisibility...

You and I, like the waking sun
new in form, each morn...

You and I
a deal on two for one
farthest heights
awed by the swaying hearts...

You and I
a sight of love for lords' life
Lightest chords
touched together in silent night...

You and I
far from the living
close to life
You and I
Shades of Red and Black
Endless, Indefinite, Infinite

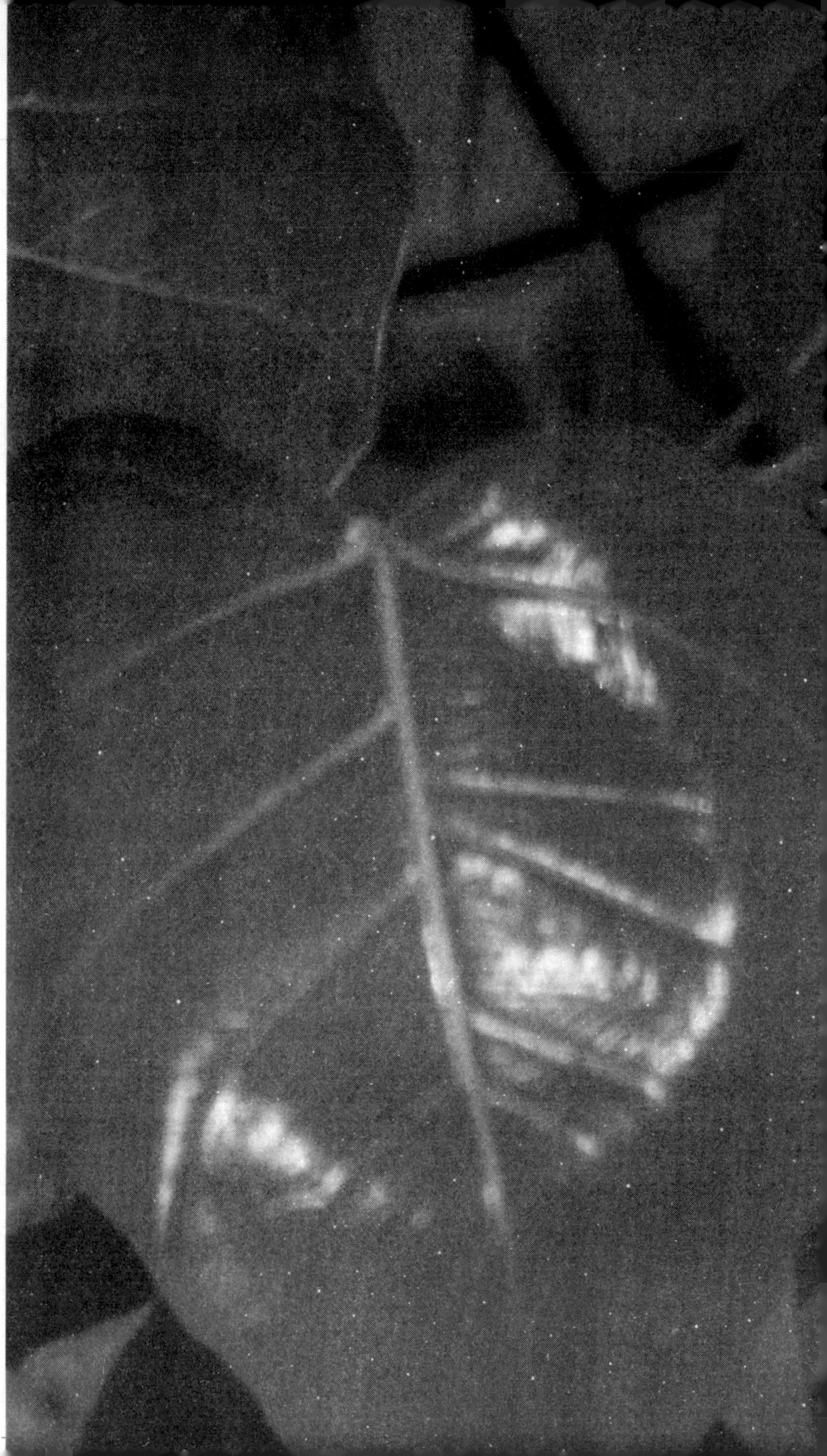

In Love Close

What is it that you say to me
that my anger brings out a smile

What is it that you do to me
that my rigidness wants to hide in the sack

What is it that your smile does to my heart
that I only want to see you when I feel low

Life gives a lot of days in a year to live
but what is it about you that my days
don't get tired running past life
and living the years off...

What is it love that you are made of
that even in my anger, and stupidity
you never let me realise where I lack
magic, mantras or super cool tantras
you surpass ocean when it goes high touching the sky

Higher than the will of the heart
deeper than the gods could place our heart
and lighter than the air that my
joys float away in my heart

I love you too mate
and I hear it too
still why is it that you making
me shout it out to my heart
aloud
that I love you and you and you and...

❑

Invisible Hands of Destiny

Destiny it was to meet you
Or was it the coincidence charted by us individually
Sub-rosa, silently

The last route it was that time took to reach love
Or was it the fate that things were to happen the way they did
sub-rosa, gradually

Totally unlikely it was for me to like someone like you
Or was it that you were everything I had never thought of that I liked you
sub-rosa, entirely

No sugar coated, no sweet words
You gave it back to me the way I did to you
Whatever that it was
Unmatched perceptions, unexpected beginnings and
Unspoken thoughts it spoke of

When you saw me
Or I thought I saw you...

❑

Just before Love

Two worlds and our pair
Getting in to a deeper mess or things are becoming
strongly clear
Story was of love and some unfound fear

One afternoon when moon shone through
And the night was discovered
He just dropped in a few words,
a praise
for all my accomplishments

As when the want surpasses the belief of not doing
Is when the heart sets our doing exactly the same thing
Care-relation was impossible to imagine
Yet with the second of a minute it got created

It was shortlived as would any object
that man can't wait to make
But which breaks on a fall

Love is never created
and cannot be attained by reasoning
It happens, just like air and rain
Runs in to you
And never runs out on you...

The way, would never exactly be known
you are strolling away in opposite direction
but love leaves you off for any amount of second not
It makes your existence a joyful journey where
You live, live, live
Only to tell
All
to let their love draw life forrad from all the fardels
for heavens and manifold cherishable rainfalls...

❑

Light in Light

Light by light as a dance in your sight
Evening call that you can't wait to stalk
Wandering hues in your mind that grows
Love that obliterates chances of solo existence

Rubbing of the eyes makes not to look easy
but it fails to diminish the colliding search of eyes

Light by light as a step in your mind
hastily all the mindfulness that we made grime

Why the hurry, why the cry
all is looked upon without a dial of lie

Wait not to start what you want to do
sleep not for that is all which will be dead and untrue

Fight by fight as a kiss by soul
feelings are beings let loose by wings so long
seen in the lonely sparkling hearts even when distance
plays its chimes from afar...

Fear never to chase your soul love
For, life will end fast coining stacks of wealthy treasures
Fear never to chase your soul love
For, life will make a hard fight to hide its truest pleasures...

❑

Lingering Shadows

In shadows, in some light
Whenever I see you, I feel so right

Why is life so subtle yet so grand
Cut it down to see its depth
In every smallest part of it love itself reveals

Life and blood
We all sometimes hail relief…

Little sand and fire
To burn us up

Little sand that forms the emotions
Makes up a look
Which when seen in another's eye
Creates smiles, dreams, relations
all other stretches beyond lips and eyes

Whisking away all the daunting
Risking giving up the fading hues
Little sand and fire

We sometimes look at and hail relief...
Hides silence not from speech
Wings you gave me oh life

Flight is mine
All limits I could breach

Little air and sand
We sometimes sink in and hail relief

Escape pains from mind too
When you get up light
Keeping away from the fright
Letting go
Of that who pushed you away
From happiness, from love, from success

Much is never needed to make happiness
Content is always a state of mind

Visualise and create we all forget to do
Obviously living in the worldly grip
of words like I, me and you.

❑

Seeping in too deep

No act, No deed,
No emotion, No consequence
No future, No newness
And everything that's living never remains unseen
By the sky
It stays, it lives, it breathes
Gazing at the ages down the lowest steeps...

Likewise mind was an empty slate
First soul left a mark which sparked the heart
Actions made, some lead fruits, some revealed stars...

What went away was not forgotten
Got passed on to another birth
Where the mission of the second soul
Was to get over with the uncompleted tasks

Each soul wrote things it wanted, learnt and achieved
in to it
And passed on
That's why the likes and dislikes and the deviations

Else how do you know which path to choose?
Or have hints of where not to go...

Your folks put forward their unattained dreams
And your soul will always whoop out to you
Your obligations by birth through its means and streams...

❑

Smaragdine Depths

Raises up to the heaven's abode
Touches the cold wants that were naked to your eyes
Turned them in to so calm
Content things
Like they were to be but pots of dried up gold

The knock of life was so received
As when given to one with vacant heals

Silently always life unfolds the Loud passions

If I were to say my luck
live on all the love given
Else in love would have to be found
A fit...

Touching is to remove distances
As does the heart when thoughts are resolved
Matches it up to that category
Where when one follows a thing
And rest builds up accurately,
The desired process

Some shape it, some are given a shape
But we all grow here by god's grace.

The beginning

From the realms of my existing soul
and the nights that were spent alone
From the swirling of water
and the falling of the rain drops
till the days quickly can come
to an end
and till the depth of my eyes can see
You and nothing else

From my longings and everyday prayers
in the want to find the love
to complete that for which I was born
till the deepest fears that my heart ever felt
would all be covered once that smile shines

From thousand different distances
to crossing the paths with you
Stretching over the years without you
to the craving for listening to your soulful voice
From the deepest heart of my soul
to the hollow realities that lay
naked without you

Knew a part of you which was
always with me

Kept a part of you which was always with me
Kept memories of you oh love
in a want to finally get you

Have lived my life to wait for you to come
to come and love me and take me home... ❑

The Final Delusion

Had long ago left your space
your memories let drown
your entity to never live around

But one afternoon it was you
who again came back
A sad happening you told the tale of…
My heart grew receptive to your words…

A new space put you towards me
and I unthinkingly stepped ahead forward

Life is not a coincidental plan
it makes sure to tell you, to show you
to whom you should belong and how and where it can
be wrong

The delusion it was of the sweetest month
the final one
in-for-you to conclude its unreal term…

❑

The Power Turn

What gives you the power to quail when lover wants you?
Who gives you the power to hurt when the
sheets over the faces are drawn?

Our night stays awake, the silence trying to
find its deepest abode
Who chooses the way to improve or let go
When fire is felt in both the hearts that stay
through the night
distanced apart...
Mocks at this time the exotic air that through
the window-open
is touching my hair...
When infinite love was sworn by our joined hearts
What gives you the power to decipher a
way anew on your own?
When the journey undertaken was
never started alone...!

How do you know the right?
When your right was supposed to be me?

The swings are empty now, night bird hails aloud
It's lover it's searching for

but the long shivery lane lies covered in
dark grey leaves, finally dried up to be crushed…
Who shall fill in the fading colours?
Who shall quail this time and hurt the other?

My love is true like the river that flows
It might create sounds unique each time,
Yet in it's heart it would always be serene…

By mere daily throw of cruel words
You concluded the desire
My breath waiting to be touched
Your steps are yet to follow…

Fear I generated in the small things that I could
otherwise deal with
As knew I, you would come smilingly
ready to remove the shackles off…

Always wanted you in my heart's bloom
It's same love-gestures now you are beginning to hate
Frustrated in love you appeared like any another
fellow
Not the same charm, not the appealing eyes
Insensitive to my touch, indifferent to my cries…

You adorn now some hard soul's gusto to live
the hard way
Nicely you sleep now
while I wait to behold and feel your
warm touch again…
In my nicety, my ego, self-respect, I forget to tend to
As you had done for me more than my eyes could
believe…

Who gives you the power to let go of me
to make me see where I was wrong?
I tell you now,
To leave me, to make me see where I went wrong
Is never the way I could ever come to see the after-
clap...

What gives you the power to quail when lover wants
you?
Who gives you the power to hurt
when the sheets over the faces are drawn..?

❑

The Silken Touch

May be I will see you when I see you
Maybe I will tremble when I will speak

May be the drops will meander through
the untreaded pathways
Maybe the meaninglessness in attempt to grow will
unfold a sense in its glory

Maybe the menorah will light up my lies
spoken at times
Maybe you will be in love enough not to see them
And maybe I will be in awe thinking of
your love all the time

May be the menu won't provide my
apple-pies sometimes
Maybe you would go far to get them

May be the writings on the standing stones
will not be washed away when we are gone...

May be this is the time I should open up to you
And maybe this is the time I should run
straight to you
and tell you that I am scared no more...

And maybe this is the life, the life we wanted to
carve for ourselves out…
Maybe there are thousand maybes
I should not be forgetting of
But baby, there is a definite maybe which
ceases not to tell me
that I want to be all yours…

❑

Tides

Love relationships when get destined
Up high in the sky
Layers are added, sweetness designed
Days are fixed, clocks set to remind...

Evolution it is one of its kind
In its sound and form, higher we can recline...

Uncertainties then are presented
thereupon to the object
Works out not then any other relationship
and for a moment, hopes and wills are let flown...

Sad-hearted souls get up and begin to follow their role
Until one day
The invisible hand picks you up again
and throws you off to the other object of
pure admiration...
Adoration follows the path
As you get to know where you were going wrong
And how you have now got all the right delights...

Learn a lot you do when in real love
Lets you be truly a beautiful person in & out
No shades of red and black where could be
searched upon...

Then no matter how far you look and what you see
It's only red, red, red,
A part of you,
A part of me...

Can't live without love then you and him
And all the comfort lies in the thoughts of uniting
after
the workfull day hits its end...

Sea it is not real love, deeper you go you
lose breath and get lost
Sky it is not real love, so far to reach
Magic and endless charm and passion it is
Once attuned to its rhythm
the melody never wears off the lips...

Tides these are of several lifetimes,
It's depth one could always feel
But it never lets you drown...

❑

Yesterday was Over

When not in love,
While looking for love

Being nothing found

Alcohol or being with the nature
are the only profound meditations
one could relish
to prevent from being hollow...

As when the motives are destined
You coincide with them by doing…

Every word uttered makes sense
And every order given falls in its own fence…

World is truly your place,
You might win it with your word(s)
But if internally strong
Can win it with your silence and grace…

When not in love
While looking for love

Being nothing found
Think profound, live life proud…

❑

Love Memoirs

When the death of a close someone or the end of love falls suddenly on our doorsteps, we are let drowned by a string of time into the larger timeline that speaks in itself and shows us the past things that have since then passed.

I wondered how some of the most talented people, who were really promising right from the school days, get directed into a bubble due to various tragic circumstances and then their dreams about making a big mark in the world becomes only about their fight to struggle for 'existence'.

How we fight schedules to sustain ourselves and how it's only the time spent with loved ones and their memories that can only keep us going on till the end. And yet god gave us this task to maintain ourselves, to earn so, no matter how material it seems, it's as important as love...

Love can't ever be replaced. If it's anything at all that fills life into a dead heart or a hurt soul, it's love.

True & Divine! True love happens once it's true, rest all are manifestations of knowing the kinds of people who exist. True love is the source that is so bestowed upon in the world like the water of the river. It has no end, no beginning. Only keeps on flowing with the endless days and nights and never-ending process of life. It might end when flowing water dissolves itself in one flow and the cosmic spirit unites but that is a day way too far.

So, those of you already having loved ones right close to you, do not be naïve or ignorant enough to start sharing joyful moments with them. Make them laugh, make yourself happy. Why not do it when they are still there? Why wait for things to happen to derive happiness from them and then become happy? Why is it a beautiful word! It questions and delivers the truth!

I have known people who have wonderful partners and yet they seek for their soul's fulfilment outside among friends, who are but merely passing strangers on the road's life map. I pity them for they will never know the warmth of those eyes felt only when the person who loves you looks at you in all the lively spirit ready to just live off the life with you and that too as you want it.

How wonderful is it to have someone you love and someone who loves you back. There are passions; they lead you to gather great accolades. There are endless hours spent working trying to shape the realities of functional bodies, they make you wise and broaden how you think. Then when you get back home or anywhere else (temple or special places of peace), you get love, this makes you want to live.

Love memoirs are memories of love that once was believed to be true. But really, love that is true by soul never leaves you alone. It stays. If it doesn't, it was never love.

❑

Love, thy charm taketh not away
in drowning
that the world ordinary
tries to shovel over with…

Broken Shadows

When broken shadows are stepped over
they mark the end of that
which you once fearfully created…

Silver linings marking the ever so growing positivism
that had long been shadowed in the sky
that overlooked my window
Many days passed, sung in the praises of
our glorious past
Our sky will change the hues that will finally come
through the broken shadows…

In-letting our souls divine, we search for
the ultimate peace
Meet alongside many good souls,
the ways of discovering lying sacred, mysterious and
unknown to eyes
eyes of our soul continue to perceive the change
that even through empty days haul on to say
that it will come…
the day will come… when we would be there…!

Sunsets now are seen with open eyes
that stare every act of the sky, seeing it carry

it's time out, do the same things
while we complain of same routine
It does the same act, without a faltering blink
Larger than life our wishes may seem
through our own windows
yet for the granting one above or within it all
that he could offer...

It's simple the rule of living this life
When heart is sought with profound
vanities that shine beyond
the already glistening curves that carry our marks
Horizons widen and lay open the serene images of
coming days
that you planned to spend with your near and
dear ones...

Life is such an arcane slip, that it is merrily felt
when halcyon days are around
and yet when you try to look back and find them
once alive vivid emotions would be vapidly on the
anvil of our sorrows be found...

The evening is withdrawing from the
clutches of the warm sun
and wanting to be free, expand a little,
spread its wings
blow away the air to those who seek the evening bliss
underneath the
ever-compassing gulmohar walks...

Shadows will haunt us of the coming times
yet in our feeling the free divine spirit inside us,
the revelling beauty of it only could let us flee...

❑

Fallings Withheld

A thread upon the wall
Sewing lying against the timeline

A joy hanging down the heart's will
Rising of emotions clinging to the hope of
finding true love

A rope up the rock
Climbing over the inhaled failures to drop
them off forever

A sound making heart
Words said never stop to allure and remembrance,
a repeated song

A bucket for a bath
Shivering well shied off from the lover,
the touches delectable

All that rises in the heart, and all that falls within
The force with which it was created by the self

Highs and lows of all the moments
Risings and drawings of all the requirements

With the nature's will we all sometimes fall
and are brought together... ❑

Felicity of a Rising

The edges run swift on the crust
Grows in the dreams, sharpening its laws
Silence evident in its curve, greater its growls

Had heard a lot about love
in the past
In its need, mighty it stays
If tried to reach, taller it will stalk

The idea of it hovers around in steps
Goes inside yet nothing would be felt
Surface has no love light

Seeing others in love, the charms
Appeared dull and bright

A pledge others do in love
Awestruck eyes cherish this pleasant do
Yet in hollowness of witnessed changes,
failing loving's
the platform-finding love does shrink
from the spaces till hopes lie due…

The edge cuts along the possibilities
that soul saves...
Looking away from the evils, mistrusts in love
My being strived to let my love reign...
Pull the act higher...
Where there are no lies, no hidden deeper sorrows

My days start and end in the look-out
for love
Almighty shall bring it along
my peace sunshine, a nightly calm
more beauty added by her divine love-string so
strong...

❑

Flickering Intellections

Reclining on the secrets will let them rest
But only till the time you want them to

Go out and respond to a call at your friend's behest...

Plans by god are heavy to re-call
Mind conceives desires,
in its claws we simply
rise and fall

Meet people we love, hate and forget
Moments get registered,
Mind plays the trick, sometimes it regrets

Whispers a monition, which we choose to flip
Unable to catch up with the spent emotions
as they roar in brutal upheaval and tuned whip

Spent mind would be best let gone with a twitch
than be saying it out to somebody
Faltering
Creating openings into a past time ditch
that will do more harm than good
trailing to a commotion of another careless mood
which will come handy for criticism
hitting harder your almost passing blues...

❑

Inklings of Lost Lover

I was walking by, not looking for a stop
Sensation called me, but far lied my hope
Absolution could have cleaned my abhorrence not
of people I chose not to like
But of people who would still leave me on
my own not…

What strength lies in the weak bodies
that
the eyes fail to see…?

Is it in your eyes
that I aim to rise but never want to be seen?

I know you
I know you care for me
yet in your kindness only restrictions I see
in-extremis I shall pray for your wellness
live in your thoughts wherein all my objections…

What happiness lies in your loud cacophony
that my joy screams of angst…?

Is it in some time that I will be regardant
critiquing my shrill individualism?

Why is it to people, as it can be with things
this duality that the man suffers from…?

Acceptance without a resolve
creates but a web of shrines whose idols are worshipped
but recognised not…

❑

Love, you said like Death

It's so amazing how people can talk
Even better as then you know
You can't talk to them…

Pretty as hell to know your drowning well
So much more of daisy-bush to collect
to get to home
Put up to show that makes light,
even silence in fragrances glow…

Words are like things and beings
When given like a blow
Hurts like the last death in a row
of re-incarnation

When given with a wing
It will make your heart sing
heals like a Sanjivani
wake the hollows that
stay hidden, embraced in our heartily shallows…

❑

Nights that hailed fear

It is not in the nature of any man to cry...

Stop believing in what you are made to believe
Cry and get it over with...

Notions created by heretics
Were so as to clear their minds off...

Why stay stuck to them notions that
Everybody made to free their self from themselves?

Creation of anything new comes from the old
Yes I would be old, if I can create new.

Stretching on aspects that disrupts a settled society...
How far would you reach by reaching the person
who was always far by heart?

Live like you thought you wanted to
For people would come and go

Dreams and love may not always be so soulful
that they would take away the crave to rest and eat...

They only give the fast pace to live and re-live your
Inner person,

Without a break, without a pause
till you attain the silent hermit's nirvana compose...

❑

Fey-some road, dainty stars

When you visit the places you loved once
With changed feelings
You contrive to create...
Nuances,
light and penetrating...

Silent and calm the evenings unfolded themselves into
the glistening hues
of their romance
no dapper no delicate dame,
they revelled daring the
horizons that were keen to expand...

Darby and Joan, they construed their love into any
category not
Evading the norms of all acknowledged forms of
behaviour
Societal acceptance they sought not...
Why seek that which their God has bestowed
carelessly upon all?

'Acceptance'

His rules are but collectively rooted in the winged soul
Engraved on the heart's golden flange,
Fractional disturbances it absorbs whispering
Peaceful mantras of life and land...

Bunch of remarks, end-ways full of haters
Could extirpate the passion from their hearts not
when they visited the places
their entities where were formed...

Challenges let alone fearful thoughts
Could frame up visions of haunting tomorrow's not...

Morn and night, in each other's blissful love
They would hide...
Fences of harsh realities could keep them in a
closure not
Good or bad, their acts were always for each other...

Even the fuddled, chaste heart
Spared itself from the fumes of the falling stars...
Stars they would find in their own sky
unspoiled, unflinching, unfettering...

Naming the days in the delights
of their corrections and errors
They would grow out of the clouds,
unto the newly found old roads...
Rains where would soak not their running
fey some dreams
Sparks would rise where
in the middle of the life's well granted streams...

When you choose to ignore that
Which has a special place in your heart
Your unwillingness, defeated dalliance
stays strong enough not to forget those
who keep revisiting your unspoken memories,
still vivid and kept by you far apart…

❑

The Black Dins

There used to be a calling in you
a night unlit by glimmering skies
its hues showcasing the gateways to fly...

Your dreams never failing you
The temptation trying to reveal the best that's due
Your hope of love, growing sweet awaiting the days
Torn altogether from the disappoints that it could slay

Your friends called you everyday
The conversations, their words
Never aimed to lead you,
Leave astray...

There used to be a meadow of long hours spent
playing
Colours of brightest zeal, lemon dipped sweets
Those moments of earned laughter in your faked up
shrills
A kiddies' zeal to climb up those highest hills
To reach where there are no sorrows, no black dins...

There was a calling in you that you now crave to feel
Your friends, your family, your school,

Your worked upon enchased skills...
There was a calling that
you can search again to sow
What you want to grow in you,
row by row

The shadows will never cease to chase
However,
You could end up the disputes in your mind
by filling in life your final peaceful shades of white...

❑

The Call on the Run

Twists returned to their natural history
Clocks took their usual turns
Eyebrows held pride
lush with drownings of the past...

Time ticked down the eyes thus
Followed the call,
which always kept the sight walled...

Heart kept running, following the call on the run
The distance, the proximity, the depth
Destinations laid accurate measure of...

Heart felt dreams, long sleeping desires
Found solace in the calls of the past
as in the longings
even a mere care could be made to last...

Swift, bothersome realities shaped to their
troublesome form
moving to the highs...

Below the lying, took shelter
my graceful resolve

Eyes held pain shivering
with my faltering greys

Soul kept searching, following the call on the run
The distance, the proximity, the depth
loose emotions making fun of
much awaited realities and childhood dated tales
dissolved in the viciousness
my world couldn't let detain
Where lies the soul
mind tries to find and chase

Random, pleasant surprises burgeoned to life
Smiles flowered to the skies
Higher the highs became
myself saw the one...
Heart knew he was close
a non-ceasing heavy love dose

The ideas of two
the fairy tales of the hoping heart
did come true...

Emotions were understood and its imprints glued
the mark of soul love was left in the heart
its divines, the magical cravings barely
getting not carved
Far, far lied my fears
the calls silenced the questioning stars...

The hills that called upon me once in search of love
Carried the presence of my love in its air
Which now only blows
Moving my hair past
As on its surface
I lie down with my mate
Our love only to last…

❑

The Cover-up

The cover-up in my earnestness
I couldn't do every time
I try and try and try
Yet in your eyes I could never be seen…

How long before the morning sun shines?
My nights speak of darkened sorrows.

Who else apart from me does it bind?
Clock, made
only to let time bind us quickly
Is doing its job not…

The jargons you gave
some we created in our laughing love
Now haunt me
I swear I am becoming shallow…

Our pagan god had brought us together
In his gentle smile
our souls attained their sheen…

Now the day has so mercilessly been passed
It speaks of evil

Of the times that I feared shall come up...
Layers of our love we had dug-in too deep
Day by day with our love
we had through the darkest days
beheld our pride and esteem...

Now you sleep away in a tired body
and I am consumed in your love
sleep I can't
without cuddling in your soul's warm touch...

A kid I had become
In the live-in journey with you
Now left alone
where to look up
I would now barely know...

Why is it to life as with good and bad times
that it brings different days and nights?

Why can't love sustain the sweetness
stay bereft of trivial nuances...?

What makes the soft smile that once
charmed the heavens
become dry and dull?
That it attracts hate, lonely nights
and loudest knocks of hell...

The cover-up in my grandest panache
I could not do every time
I try and try and try
Yet in your eyes
I could never be seen...

❑

The Covetous Love

Once the pain is left alone not
The lost love fades away from
Baleful nights not...

Impatient tidings ruling the turned life
Caustic, reactive emotions of you
Push my strife beyond the tolerable shores...

How a cause when spoken to another
takes small time
in each of its described second whisper
hours of subdued, corroding pain
it shivers...

Lights are turned off now,
Last curtain has been drawn
My best last smile darkens
Struggles through the vacant
left over nights...

Covetous, hard to sought
You are oh love,
My deepest desires you have touched and
quietly cut out...

My boisterous charm and gleaming looks
Is following its plan
to propose to all
one love-sick belief
making everybody believe...

Hope lies against hope
the cantankerous strings of my
suppressed howls and shouts come out
in the hours that fade to elope...

Night continues to carry my misery
to the ends of unrecognized sea
A name, I could not give to your
curt and love reply...

Tides, beautiful and high,
sweep my awkwardly beheld thoughts of you
in nicety, seeping into my
strings of heart and its leads...

Clouds hover around the stars
Air not caressing enough to make them move
stay and fight back the clouds...

Yes, love you are oh strength
Delineating conduct through your
mightiest appeal...

My lonesome soul descrying through,
the forgotten dreams...
what lay there precious
where velvety glances met and love it gleamed...

Morning hour awakes my curmudgeon
self once again...
time to earn for life now...
My frailties I myself try to deceive...

Alas the night has been allowed
to let pass...
The openings, new and strange befall
Upon the shrills of telling time
That kindles and discretely
withdraws...

❑

The Last Solace

Wat lays forgotten lies far beneath
Forget heart can't what it sow
A look when falls on the life now so raw…

Cries out heart, seeks no existence
And ripped stands life
devoid of soul…

When the last solace draws black upon the hopes
Life complicates,
Love falls
And the world drowns…

Nothing changes the will of a dead soul
No more the scarings
as would haunt the scattered lot…

Nothing comes when sole reason to live shatters
No sound, no words
coming out of the mouth stands true
when the last solace draws black on blue…

What lies ahead cannot be the same
life after all proved to be a pain…

How all wishes can come true was often
the thought of the innocent heart…

Now after ages, the life has become dull
It's shine restorative by none…

How to sit up and how to look
just wish could turn to the ages of two…

The last solace
had his heart belonged to another…

The words now banging in my head forever
hurt am not, nor am I sad
ripped I am of the soul I had once felt…

They say
As you sow, so you reap…
life played again its old game
coined a fool with a love petal name…

Silence of the creation is met with
when the last solace
leaves you alone amidst the creeps…

It was just a beginning, a realization crew
never knew it would strike so hard in the heart
with the pain drops,
coated blue…

Writing, oh solace I now name you
take me back to times when I was not created
My love, my trust, my faith when lay not insulted…

Call me back to you, take me along with you,
make me smile
and say to me
go live your life...

When you have found a reason for me here
when you can heal my heart which lies open
take me back...
this is not me, cannot be me...

Take me back to the ages of two
and send me afar
where nothing feels blue...

❑

Visited

Silent I was lying in my bed
letting free time to lead...

Through a deep melancholy of moments lived
came along images, smiles, laughter
fears in black and red...

Stayed on voices in the ears
and some words which were hard to forget...

Passion led life swirled down the lips
came along a call
and life differed little from its plight...

While visited me all this while
came to my dimly lit room
only the moon of the great night sky
whose comings I could never ever deny...

❑

Wrong

From time to time, I need to speak
of how I go wrong
but can never see…

Life, you would remain a mystery!

The day I think I got down to working
and now would understand
things appeared haywire…

You brought back a face
which was once liked
No will to go back now
where in the past
I could never walk…

From time to time, I need to speak
of how I go wrong
but can never see…

From time to time, I need to see
Who I am from inside
But truly to one person
I could never reveal…

Love's Beyond

'Love's Beyond' is the phase one reaches in love where they know that their love can never change and what it should not be now that they have truly wholly known their lover.

Love goes through many phases and incites in each one of us some change as well. The changes sometimes might be restrictive on you and, on the other hand, sometimes they might just be the gateways to freedom.

Love becomes restrictive when too many conditions are laid down on your lover simply because you have high expectations from them. Where you might be thinking of making them or transforming them into wonderful human beings capable of managing all and yet, in your determined spirit, you might also be giving too much to your lover than they could take.

Love becomes a gateway of freedom when your give you lover ample space and time, so much that you are so close yet the space that you own as a person is not crashed down as well. This is the sweetest gesture anybody could do for the ones they truly love.

Why always tell what they can do or direct or guide them? They didn't fall in love because they wanted a mentor. They simply need love which is as simple as drinking water. And yet in all our complexities we make it seem so tough. Why? Whom does it please?

'Love's Beyond' is the state of celebration of love where your soul knows that your love will remain unchanged in spite of anything external that falls upon.

It's a feeling of supreme understanding that extends with an honest and not a compromised smile to your lover. 'Love's Beyond' is every aspect of your inner soul that has realized its love for life in one person and simply would stay in love 'beyond' all other reasons or whims of mind.

❑

When I am drowning oh love into the sea of love
behold my soul along with yours
and plunge deep into the ocean called life
and reach to me through the medium called Love...

Affection, not love's name

Love is not about trying to like somebody
because they are nice,
It's liking somebody so much
that you wouldn't want anybody else
than that person...

Sliding doors slowly shifted the focus on to you
You appeared engrossed in your world,
while the real one in my ideal world
seemed to matter very little...

What is real is still unknown in the ever charming rays
of this evening sun...

Through the corridors of my sweet escapes
it had all begun...

Walls were painted in red and white,
You sat there carving what was probably lost in time...
Somebody's unseen eyes...
Must be the loneliness shining through the whites
that my heart so red absorbed all your lifeless quiets...

A love arose from the sadness of your being
I came and sat by your side...
Did you just smile and raise heaven's pride...?

A soul, loveable I found you to be
lost in times of a grown up world...
What all can you carve out?
How much will you draw,
before this evening sun goes out,
it's our path you got to line out...

Dark grey passions emerging in the sky
all becoming dark
even the colours in red and white
You looked at me closely
my beauty surpassing your lost times...

Don't be in awe oh lover
For its' time I cheated
and came by through a lie...
To help you live
my nightly intention...

When you held me closer
It's affection for you that made me hover

Night remains night
Only so it can yield stars
and not so that through its own darkness
it could one day rise...

Such was my affection for you
which in the name of love
I accepted first
It's fallings along with time
I had to ultimately let die...

❑

Bereft of Wailing

Do not wait so much for things to happen,
Try first and then wait a while...

Story was of love that happened in its full delight
It had faces that were in heart being searched for day
and night...

Direct was never the look and the desire to get
together
in the opposition however lay all the sweetest
treasures...

Surprising it is with things as it's with love
When not sought, comes right to you
Stays off-edge when looked for and searched upon...

Too much push-on is the strangest human emotion
Get rid of it to better the trauma...
Less the pain one goes through finding love
Patience seeps in...

Why wait for her to step your way?
When kinship speaking through the evening
didn't let the charm to fade away...

Easiest it is to fall in love in with a friend
yet, when rushed
after listening to others teasing words
barely could one hold the butterflies
the sweet hushed flush...

So, why wait a while when the path has become visible?
Why think more every now and then,
when the complex mind has come to a conclusion...?

❑

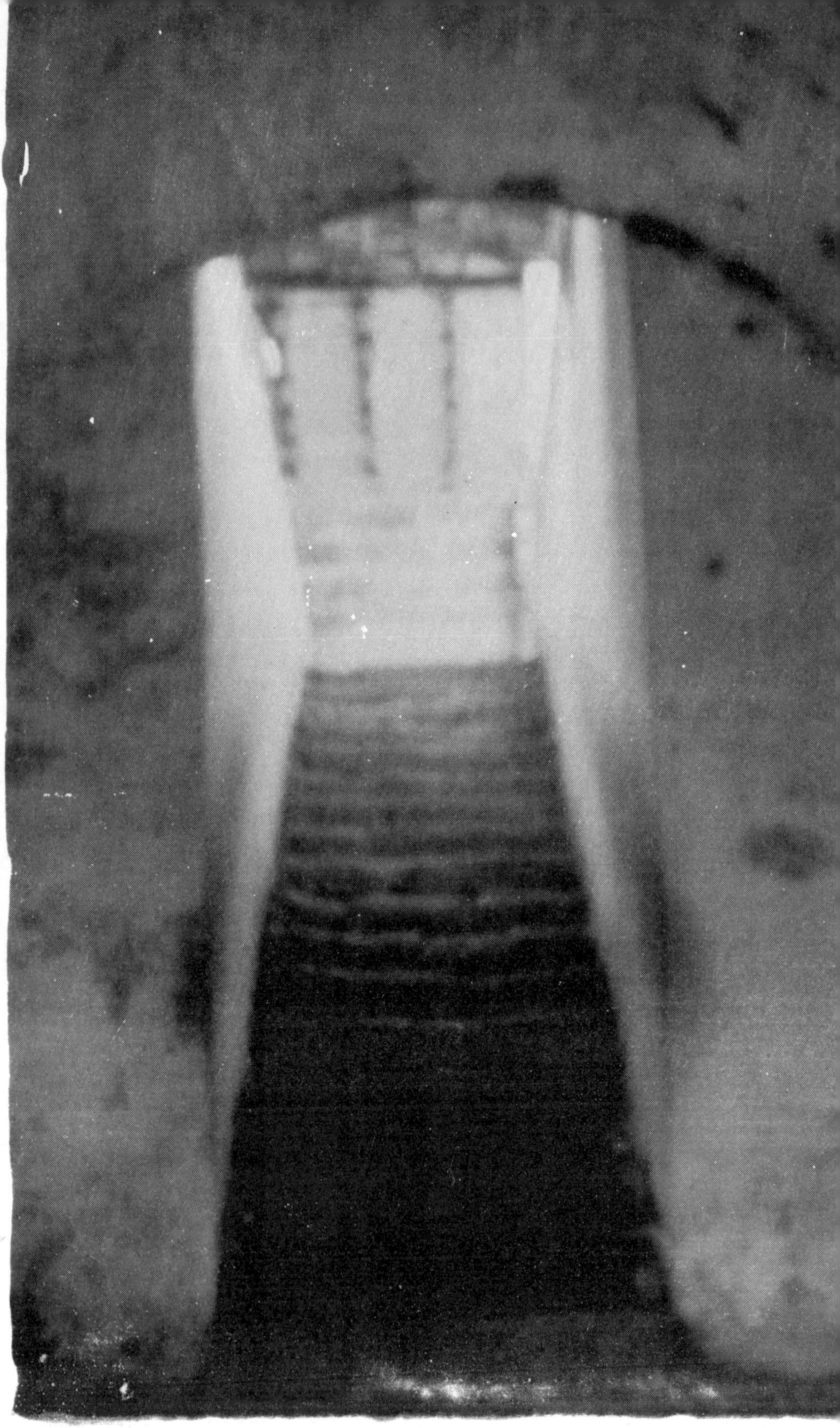

Equation of Love

When placed at a distance,
Differences are appreciated much closely…

Distance is a myth
and myth subsides in light of truth never…
Just like when in love
The hues of tense clouds look plump and ready to always fall…

In the sky
several settled clouds forgetting their colour and depth
throughout the days
contain water and then sometimes fall
unchaining their colour and depth
meandering through the shuffles of the teasing air…

On the earth
millions of broken, mend up hearts
embracing the sorrows that now seems to be their own bodily part
Cut out can't this heart
the experiences of known likeliness
Once in love tries to keep all the evils apart…

When in love that could wait for years at end
do not make time a factor of your decision...
As your hastiness would only reveal a lost charm
but if lived through pink times
could heavenly let your love prosper...

Distance is an illusion, really
where stand on footing the laces of those
tear-filled eyes
like collected drops of rains coming together to
survive...

Cherish the distance
see how far the calling winds allure...

Talk to silence
sent by the love rising from the place you once left...

Go back to her you traveller off shore for
the evenings would always continue to haul...

How far you will tread your watery way?
The end of water's land
shall soon haunt you to go back several miles
where lies your real home...

where you have through the lens of differences
tried to see each in better sun...
Lights in your eyes never spoke the lies
then why wait more
and burn these lonely nights...?

Distances are really well meant to be broken by those
who once lived in love and never missed the world...

❑

Eternal love-name

Careless sweet gestures make
well thought-about lavish endeavours coy

Enough has been said now oh maya
my love is not a shadow searching its truth…

Your charm has named my nights in their clouds
the journey has now started…
Our love newly found…

New is nothing here
but a part of the plan
yet in our small occupied frames
our dualities do better living than our beating hearts

If I could indeed rule my heart with my love
I would not be waiting for the moment to show its
light…

Enough people of your kin have said now
my love is at stake
fire has been set
Could you in your earnestness bring the well
sought ring

before the ashes would need to be drowned…?
Yes, love is beyond the world's journey
hold my soul and catch me by your love
Distance I shall tread, farther from this
hatred-filled life…
Farther from evil that is present only to
destroy love like ours
come and behold Maya,
your love is in the air for once
it's your day and rain has its promises beheld

Just follow my words as they reach your heart
the shackles would therein only unlock…
Barren, dry life is nobody's destined abode
Why should not we make one little cue and cord?

Your whispers reaching my shivering soul
My deciphered clues,
Your liberating sojourn…

It's the morn that should show your smile now
I pick up the fallen strands of spent emotions in
your wait
Locked are my flying angels away in their kingdom
I look at them from my room window and their
laughter I see
drowned in melodies of unforeseen times
they tell me to believe in and wait…

If I could wait, my love shall prove false
My Maya stays awake, some courage I must exhibit
to bring the lady love back to where she would

carelessly dream her visions of a beautiful life
Day light took me to the door that caged you
No dark nights I needed for my love was nothing full of shallow
From behind the door, you looked at me in tears
My heart relieved
for it was there to end the sorrow...
The kin revolted and practised several blows
I took it all till my blood itself would stop its flow
They took pity on my courage so low...

Well thought-about lavish endeavours
make careless sweet gestures of love coy...
My love spoke for me when my courage knew
no solace but only the resolve...

If blows had bled me to death
I would have come back for you
and taken you with pride

My love is not weak
Why in their mercy shall it ever reside?

Oh Maya, you threw me in a rose bush
The thorns bled me
but the petals had me blushing with your
blooming cheeks...
Our love could stand strong
Where the lanterns could burn in the
light of love not...

Yet the energy of our love had the power
that surpassed all those who were touched by it
Knew we always that sudden was our love plan...
In this god's world indeed
nothing ever happens unplanned...

❑

Five on You

Five on you,
like the building blocks
Take me high, from the lie drawn far

Put in you,
that trust in your love
Search me up,
from the shallows you pulled me by

Five on you,
like crossing fingers
Feel me deep,
surfaces where fail to reveal

Hide in you,
like the last solace
listen me up, whispers when are carelessly dropped

Five on you, five on me
Fingers crossed, a staircase to flee
High hopes, much higher levels we see

High hopes, much higher levels we see
Dew drops where shine up to last,
skipping their falling spree...

❑

Love Against the Plans

More you provoke and tease oh destiny,
more prone I become to your schemes
So bring it on till you find your buried down
ocean in the deeps…

A chance at love you gave me
I couldn't any more complain
Initial charms were the best of all
Could never let me see the real shades
Magical it seemed
a mere coincidence planted by you in my heart
Mind stopped to work
Logic ran away to its own darks
Soon I realized how to pick myself up
from the puddle of namely love
Lighter the soul grew day by day
in its pain it yelled at me
close your eyes to the false pretences
wake up truly to the morning light

I gathered my strength
My family giving enough of love
I could see between red and grey
And no traces of black

Now heart determined to clog in its love tray
Only red and love and love and faith
that could please the heart
and rejoice in my saintly serenade...

Strong and independent was the way chosen
by my soul
as it had heard your voices
wanting me to explore to rise and somewhere belong

I took the new path where my soul cherished
the glory of my efforts
Innocent heart looking for love
maintained its achieved silence

I reigned in my self-created world
No faltering steps I could trace
Nothing that was left undone

Love wasn't exactly that was on my mind
when the stars probably took a different path in
the zodiac
The skies showed the way
and brought you my way
I wasn't ready for love oh destiny
yet you gave it to me
Sudden your ways, sudden your gifts
An eye is needed that has lived through the times
to receive your blessed gift
I had the eye and the heart
yet in wait of right time someday
One day suddenly the right moment you gave out...

I would never blame you for doing the
wrongs oh destiny
as without them I would have never really
understood your plans...

Love Binds, Kind Eyes

A girl says to her love,
step up through the eyes,
smile up the quilt..

Wonderful beginning she had in a sweetest month
Where the antics of her lover ceased to succumb
Each time they met
Antsy, charmed through the waiting hours she smiling sat
When lover came, he got the delectable surprises
Things when come with love
double the mirth leading to unnoticeable neatly done compromises

Time flew away with the festivity of my being in a new love
Final one she had called it in her heart...

Doubts she had yet,
when would he finally pronounce it to all
Day by day her anticipations found no trail of the day she envisioned
In his business with a smile and a hug
she always managed to glisten

like the ice of the sweetest delirium
before the heat melts it in jest

The sky that has stars
beholds light through the days of misery as well...

She looked in the mirror and saw a girl
Pretty like the rain's wetting drops
like a flower that bloomed through the rough
weather's blow...
Her trust misled her ending the love so sweet
Alas he belonged to the world, she thought
Not with me!

I am but a soul in sorrow
And would still continue to gleam
As the heart that beats within knows no redeem
It only brings itself up
waiting for the truest feeling
that makes us,
in any moment without a hollow mien...

❑

Pensive Deliriums in Love

What is the chase of that purpose
which doesn't coincide with the pursuit of
happiness?

The hasty steps that crawled into your lost dreams
Locking hands of yours with a fresh lover
Smiling just to believe you are happy
falling to the trap of old age love formula
Why would love be sought in the name of a need
when need is anything
but want of feeling an emotion?

Yes, time you are losing by
The hindsight growing tired, swollen
You saw a person with a delightful smile...
Yes, your puppet is ready!

Go strike on your put together charm and dose
To what extent desperateness leads the ways of nights
that in the morning you are ready to overlook all that
needs a careful hearty eye?

You were once beautiful
now loaded with wine and addictive habit of partner finding
you portray a woman who could for herself
never let anybody stay for a longer time...
Why is it that you tried hard to coin in the best of the lot
When in front of your eyes waited a person
who could love you a lot?

What did you ever get out of the endless clever means
simply when you could have enjoyed someone's love serene...

Time you feel has become right now
When you fished in your fresh lover
Lady, please stop the clock
as it is far from making its final stop
Your destination was never no purpose driven
then why dip love in the name of need
and embark on a journey wastefully driven...

❑

Raging Miles

Far treading distances
are shallower than longing hearts...

The miles have started now
that take me to you
I sit here beside this young kid in the bus
that looks at this lost lover by his side
curious to look outside
we end up changing sides...

How easily we do things for a small child
No ego comes in
No self ever contemplates and denies

I look at his eyes blinking at the fading sun
far the sun goes, his eyes keeping its run
The mountains and their air are becoming still
just like my moments when not with you

The layers in the mountains becoming orange
due to the gifted light of the leaving sun
The kid marvels at the rainbow of the leaving sun
in each layer a different new world he points at
and makes me to acknowledge his pun

I think of you when I smile at his innocent words
that's how you looked at the world
when you sat beside me in this world
Kid you were always to my grown up self
I could perhaps live a bit like a kid myself
when you laughed at crazy things I did
to lighten up your quest...

Night is falling in now
the kid is long asleep
I stare at the stars through the window
waiting to reach your doorsteps in all the impatience
You must also be thinking of me
as I could feel my heart beating louder
In my retrospection it's you
Who I fondly carried everywhere
I laid my steps and will and forgotten arrows...

The air, now dense with water that has seeped into it
is becoming cold
as I close the window
I try not to make a noise
kid sleeps gently
taking all my happy dreams to reach to you...

I close my eyes too
waiting for the morning sun to show up again
where the kid would marvel at the light
and the colours it brings
where the skies would fall down
and I would be up in the air
when I would see you waiting for me
our meeting now never
coming to an uncertainly end...

❑

Rough Waters

A wish is mine and a wish is yours
what I do calling my own reflects
you oh love
a part of me alone where I get to see not

How is it to rays, that form the surface shine
that steps of you into the chamber of my fallen wills
changed the demeanour that through the
broken glasses
could be with even closed eyes seen
as visible lay the shattered occurrences breaking the
sky in me
taking small parts where rain reserved its
essence once...

You walked in, like the shades of rainbow descended
merging two souls long lost...

In the struggle to find love
had gone through the rough waters
our steps left marks in the stream
screaming for fresher terrains to go to
drenched lies now the joy cuddling in its small bubble
says it to me often, my tenure is unbroken...

A dream chased you are and a wish was mine
What I see coming through my own eyes
is the vision of you oh love,
tomorrow's where without you I cannot see…

Day by day the limit gets puzzled in the hollowness
of its length
for, far we are from any bounding territories of our
horrifying self
Eyes meet yours like the ocean just ran off from its
highest wave
beholding its magnanimous serenity in your eyes…

You see far…
Are you the time that I was looking at
through the window of my room that I never
even through the winds could ever close?

True, hopes of anything true can never be closed down
within the heart that stays open
even when it has to be forced
to stay close and put up a display for others
the 'close ones'
around…

Not always the words we have to use with others
are such that they would mean something, anything…

Words, I will give you not, for they might with time
be forgotten
A look of my eye I present you, that rises up
to look at your face
shall never fade away in time
just like the water stops flowing not…

It moves only to move, never to stop
it moves to dissolve, never to leave
such is my love, never ending, never will decease

What I foresee judging my own instincts
is the power given by your love
alone when I was,
I could see the future in my dreams not
as the Universe was sending
its vibrational powers to my closed soul not...

Now you are here, my strength has found its source
radiate it will to the receiving energy that through the
universe
befalls upon my soul
decipher I could divinely as my god wants me to
the future of us all
My will
it would find its planet and realm
that I am sure of...

Your love will help me be
where my soul never could be...

Surrender to love, the truest of all
and ever staying
reveals a source through which
you shall continue to rise
even when the contrary might seem its result...

❑

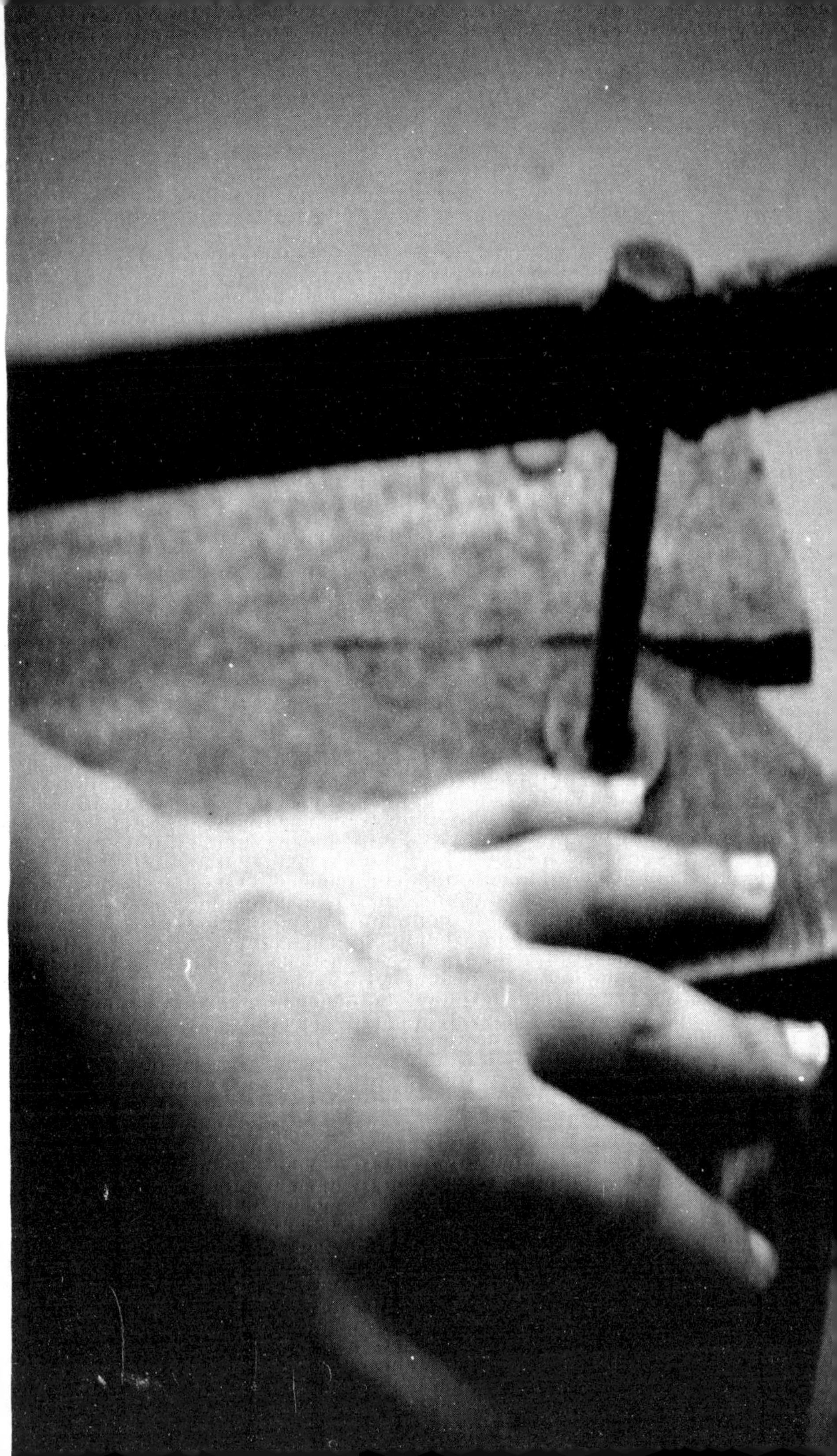

The Charted Meet

Envious of thy face of love,
Elots of charm and light and shine...

One day my eyes caught the glimpse that was of you
It sent to me your schemes even when I didn't
dare to know...

Falling in love wasn't that month's charted due
In the summer light
While catching my far off fallen star
it was then when I saw you love...

I had images in my heart
Always I drew them apart

Alluring yes your touches were
yourself that rose from the drops that dropped dead
from the plight that struck them...
Heavens sent you to enliven the moments set in
trouble...

You are still not mine
and I know not what the forest calls in their
green fallen cloaks hiding in it's shalom

you call me day and night, to the place
that goes away from my eyes not...

Heart now lives with the eyes that once saw you
Ceases it not to draw our love images still so vivid
Calls me to the places, day and night where I once
saw you...

What was the day when we had met?
What was that moment when you had charmed?
Perhaps I would never know that
since your smile, your mark I left afar...
Still chases me that evening boat till the shore
which you helped me to climb in hue and cry...
Was that the smile that through the thickest time
shone through
or was it the assurance that someday you
would finally
find me again and come through...

Heart thinks of the day when it met you
When would the sea call me again, I wait
guessing the incessant clues...
Perhaps one memory would start this journey
Where in the world-carnival for final time
I would cross you...

❑

The Warehouse of Beyond

The warehouse of memories is moving down
the forgotten stairs down the ages...
that were spent contemplating that
which once shined out of moon's sudden generosity
its entity that fell into the shape of obsession
with faint alacrity
now lying like fallen leaves, broken enough yet
not be bothered by anybody's footsteps...

The stepping stone of my tomorrow is shivering with
the burden of the dues I am to deliver
eyes are becoming small of light that could out of love
shine through them
weaker body, tired breathing routine hisses
its sentiments
of the time long gone by...

Sleeping body of mine over my bed is now just a
memory so is this life
so still like the damp sand, refusing to move...

Sun is burning in my eyes without taking its turn
yet my will shouts at me through the winds that
hung on to my body like the clamps

Unable to remove them, I struggled still
to break mirrors that showed you lies
as deep below where the shivers fell, my love
awaited your eye
a look due to rise from your eye on to mine
a night coming up with ocean's hail and length
we would give away our sorrows to the lost time
as it would behold the emptiness in its days
and give us a bit of them only through some of the
bad dreams...

Yes, struggle it is not love
yet struggle it is
to be able to finally soak your soul in another's
heart so huge
plunge into the rill that does not have a
stream outward...

When the blank spaces of time are chased
Words spread on to form their own entities...

❑❑❑